AF577221

TEO SAVORY / TRANSITIONS

Teo Savory

TRANSITIONS

Unicorn Press

Library of Congress Number 71-134749
Standard Book Number 0-87775-015-7

Some of these poems had previous appearances in *The Catholic Worker*, edited by Dorothy Day, *Monk's Pond*, edited by Thomas Merton and *Unicorn Folio*, edited by Alan Brilliant.

Woodcut on Page Twenty-three by VO-DINH

UNICORN PRESS P.O. BOX 1469
SANTA BARBARA, CALIF. 93102

CONTENTS

I. *Ten Poems for Rudy*

Ash Wednesday Poem 5
The Peregrine 6
The Three and One 7
Remembering Camus 8
In A Dream 9
Sign 10
Naming the Birds 11
Threshold Guardian 12
The Water-Pourer 13
The Quest 14

II. *Four Poems for Vietnamese Friends*

Brown Into Green 17
The Sunken Bell 18
The Children Come 20
"One Stood Waiting . . ." 22

I

Ten Poems for Rudy

ASH WEDNESDAY POEM

Kaspar Hauser died at evening:
Remember, O Man.

Lion sometimes lay with lamb
But never man of different hue
With man.

The Buddhist's bell no longer rings:
Remember, O man.

The table now is spread,
The bread is broken:
Man to man.

THE PEREGRINE

The peregrine is a tiercel and a
tiercel is not a falcon: fierce
male bird, gold-plumed predator,
swift traveler, swooping, our
golden grail, hiding deep in
hilltop forests; his eye a sphere
weighs ten times more than mine
or yours: sees a mile: reflects
gold wheat-ears, high thin sky.
'Many die on their backs,' in-
sanely clutching at their own
sky, convulsed, feathers burnt,
talons withered, from the
poisoned pollen: quest's end
now. This lapwing dead
near that thrush, two shrunken
walnuts, into dust at a touch,
our planet dead as Mars.
Yet still with a certain beauty
here, in a golden afterglow

THE THREE AND ONE

Rocks they were, the three women
having lived through much until
ageless yet still to be surprised.
He was the flash of mercury, thread-
ing from this group to that then
clotting before one for a time
a dazzling sphere solid after
fluidity. Not their finger or stick
to move this or change it yet
they had always loved him and
their eyes enjoyed flit and dazzle,
were his point of propulsion. This
was known from his darting looks
over one shoulder or between fingers his
only solidity theirs. So their sur-
prise came at his denial after
these ages when he refused them place
or grace. Rocks imploded and
crumbled and shining sphere ran out
into a thin skin of quicksilver
powerless and one-dimensional.

REMEMBERING CAMUS

His the better way: head-on
into an oak tree. After ten years
the crash is louder more grind-
ing takes an eternity, a new
Sysiphus is born into limbo
eternally crashing, eternally
smashed, his durable body
forever rooted by boars'
tusks sniffing out truffles.
Having seen
all to come
having known
the balancing act
to be worthless over a void
that the words were said the
vision enacted the myth
superseded: his way the better.
The green from the grave may
wither unwatered, but the
living corpse trampled by
hoofs is home for ant-
swarms and the bees
have shot up to the sky,
tracers for future events.

IN A DREAM

In a dream, death came.
Vision was a depthless rectangle
framed in darkness, he stood greyer
at one side of that grey screen.

What summoned him:
That day's cup of rage
or jolt of doubt, the nearer
cry of an Eastern people.

What did he look like:
He stood stiff and still,
in pose an anatomical chart,
but no veins or sinews showing—

he was all greyness. Near waking,
I saw he was made of someone's
shadow. Now, wakened, I wonder
what will summon substance.

SIGN

I am a hostage of your love
whim of your everyday eternity
when will you send your dove
and let me go? I dreamt of
mountains in Sikkim or Tibet
but found my hermitage
in low hills where peas grew
late after April snow yet the land
sustained But in the end we were hungry
in a way you cannot know and
we moved to this flat plain where
the sun circles the horizon silhouetting
tips of cactus spikes and sparks
the ruby eyes of lizards in a spread
of desolation Now I wait only for
night's fall and your feathered emblem

NAMING THE BIRDS

to Claire Trotter

Old, tattered, broken-toothed, he stood
looking a scarecrow, acting its antithesis.
On his arm, a yellow-hammer,
on his hand, a nuthatch, wax-
wings aurioled his head. The shadow
of a hemlock branch fell dense across
his hummocked face, a tree-stump
several paces distant hid
his shack. A low ridge of these
foothills hid my car and camera.
I stood in my new hunter's jacket,
quiet at the wood's edge.
A bluejay screamed, then lit
on that human tree. You too
could have them close, he
said, and named them all.
Hold out your arms, he said,
and when I did a waxwing
with feathered rustle and
no more weight than a tracery
of frost on glass paused one instant only
before going, yet here in this viewless
room stifled again by winter dark I still
feel the imprint of its claw.

THRESHOLD GUARDIAN

Night shudders at the doorway
and cannot come in barred
from entry by this uninvited
animal who crouches there
eternal guardian of my thresh
hold And I am sick of day
Rat's teeth he has snarling my night
away and a ridged tail to
threaten me Here near to hand's
this homely poker by my hearth
stone But the first stroke
must kill or it's I who'll be
the victim Night waits
the poker's raised and yet
I pause: I know my wish
yet do not know from what
or why this animal guards me
or what his purpose is
The poker falls night falters
and I stand perplexed by daylight

THE WATER-POURER

The dog leaping about his feet urges him through
woods' darkness and the scuffle of deep-veined leaves
till at the clearing's edge where moonlight flickers
he sees by its bared teeth that this companion
is a glossy fox snarling him into place
halfway toward the silent pool Here he stands
in his own silence as the woman there (her flesh
sheltered only by the beams) lowers the ewer
from her shoulder to fill it from the gleaming pool
that deeply cleaves the earth at this tree-encircled
spot with water cold and silent as the beams
that light it She could not spill one drop but
could fill her cup and the liquid neither
offered nor withheld is his to drink ten strides
away To cross that clearing is a distant journey
Near her he feels no flush or wish to touch
the perfect flesh but only thirst for what
is in her cup He drinks and it is wine
that cools his throat and burns his vision
Now she is gone and in a sunless spot
the pool lies shallow filled with
rubbish from bare trees He walks to the cliff's
edge and lies down His eyes are clear
and can look far Under his tongue
the taste of wine and burning lime

THE QUEST

Who is there now to dance with Shiva?
His dancing grounds were polished stones
laid below the altar-rock, his feet
were planted solid there, firm from earth
he'd tilled at springtime with his brothers,
and like tree-roots holding up trunk and
branches, stood him before the sacred Host,
he at worship, then making gift of it
to us, the needy he's now left behind.
He left his silence and his sanctuary
on a quest for the grail of hope,
for brotherhood from East to West,
but no one knows now what he found
or what he might have brought.
Mercy to us living, Thomas Merton,
give light to us these blind-worms
in the dark night of our days:
Teach us how to dance with Shiva.

1 January 1969

II

Four Poems for Vietnamese Friends

BROWN INTO GREEN

After five months of drought
    the rain

Hills burnt brown soil lost heart
trees in a wind danced macabre
skeletal out of season their leaves
clacking around their feet like
knuckle-bones eyes ached for green
hands for a clod of damped earth

Now the rain
    it falls gently
        beginning at dawn
            darkening daylight
    gently on roof-tiles
        in drum-drops off eaves
            gorging the ground

the rain

    falling gently outside
        lulling safe dreamers to lateness
    falling in puddles for birds
        in splashes for children walking to school
            slanting its writing on window-panes
    turning hollowed herb-stalks
        to quintessence of green

the rain

        into the deep green of our country
            where only the willow turns tender as rice

the rain

    brown into green
        will it rain
            on Hué or Phuong Boi?

THE SUNKEN BELL

The bell sounds in the temple
one strike to mark the last
of the five divisions of night
chant hope for another day
Light strikes the gold-bright
spire birds wheel and fly
away Their song makes dawn
The poem flies upward praising
the day

        The bell is sunken
under the lake water
it is slimed and dumb
In the room many are
seated around one
Outside the drenched man
green-scummed has forgot
how to walk heavy limbs
water-logged trunk Two
others dry as the earth
must drag this dredged
one between them close
to the wide glass door
In the room the chant is
low there is no bell
The door cannot be opened
fingers slither on glass
and sink The poem has flown
away

At the last of the five
divisions voices rise in the dark
birds wheel in the dark
the poem seeks the day
In the lake the sunken
bell throbs and strikes
one muffled note The earth
trembles at its stroke
The voices chant in praise
of night

THE CHILDREN COME

The children have come from Phuong Boi

The stone house is ready the Delaware
River flows by speckled with coins of ice
the pumpkins have turned and been
cut Candles within show their mouth and their eyes
apples are russet for bobbing The tow-heads
are noisy at play The two darker ones silent
and still Their more delicate hands are folded

The children have come from Phuong Boi

When they came from Suchow and Amoy
it was summer Grain was tucked into
sheaves We danced in the barn Fiddles squeaked
lanterns blackened their chimneys Hunt the slipper
came at the end and that ended with prizes
Theirs had been stamped: Made in Japan They
stamped them into the floor then sat in silence

The children have come from Phuong Boi

Once they came to the house by the Wye
There was snow and their clothes were too
thin The bonfire lit up their thin cockney
faces They shouted at sight of the Guy
burning bright as a city Their country cousins
made fun of their voices till the Guy
went up in the sky in a tall flat-topped cloud

The children have come from Phuong Boi

When they came from the towns in Japan
some gave money at sight of their skin
Never more Never more but now they've come
once again and two women for making a
protest are locked in a cell They spend three
nights with four other women all of them black
who say they've got children themselves at home

The children have come from Phuong Boi

"One Stood Waiting . . ."

One stood waiting while
the other went.
One stood crying
while the other slept.
Words with wings,
yellow-tipped,
like an erne's
from the sea, take
the waiting hours
from you to me.

DEEPDENE MONOTYPE SET BY MACKENZIE & HARRIS, HAND-PRINTED BY ERIC SMITH AND TYPOGRAPHY BY ALAN BRILLIANT.

ONE THOUSAND COPIES HAVE BEEN PRINTED, OF WHICH TWENTY-SIX CLOTH ARE HAND-BOUND BY KAREN MEECE AND LETTERED A-Z AND SIGNED BY TEO SAVORY.